That Is Symmetry!

Contents

Make a Heart 2

Look at the Butterfly 6

Paint a Butterfly 8

Look at the Leaf 10

Paint a Leaf 12

Do You See Symmetry? . . . 14

You can make a heart.

1. Fold the paper in half.

2. Draw a shape like this along the fold.

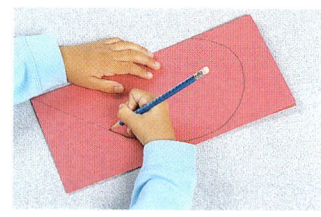

3. Cut it out.

4. Open it up.
What do you see?

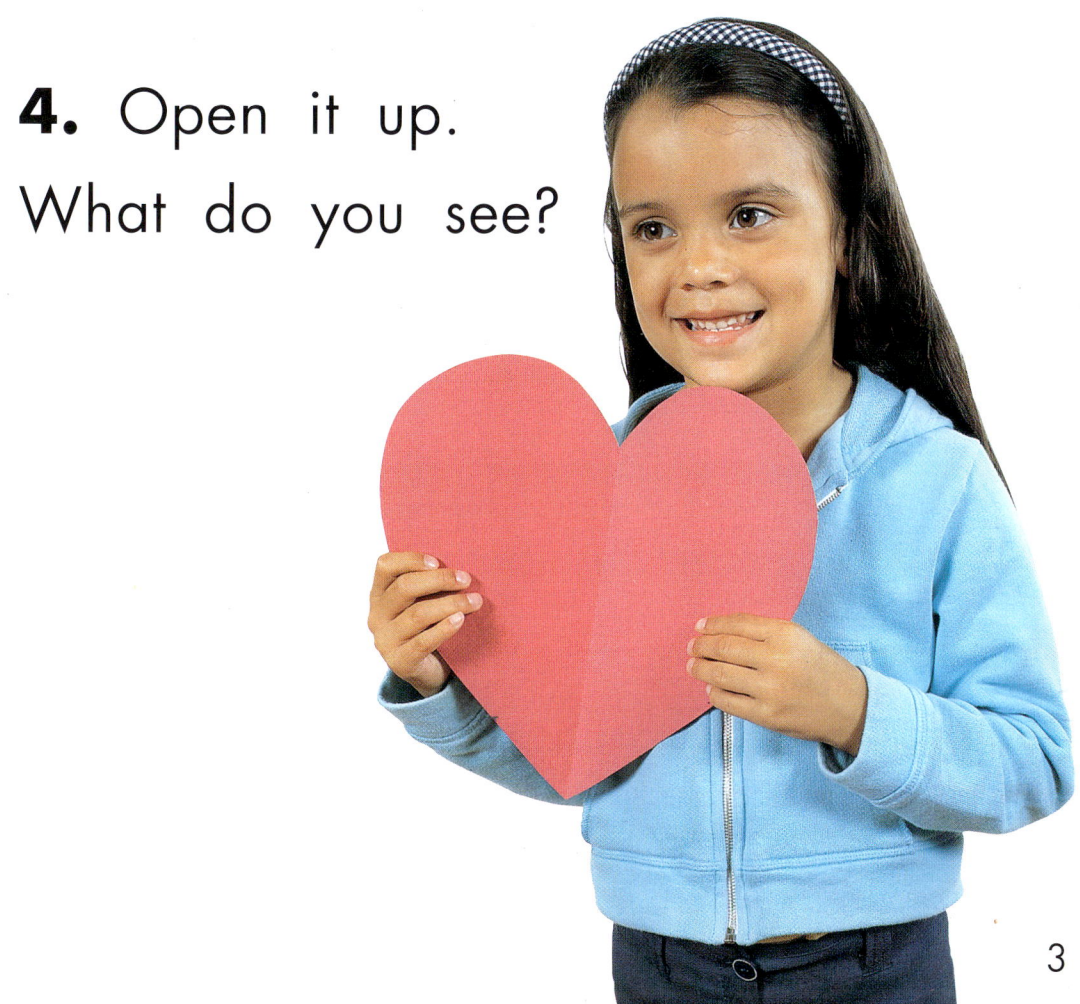

The two sides are the same.
They match!
We call that symmetry.

Look at the butterfly.
Put your finger in the middle.

The two sides are the same.
They match!

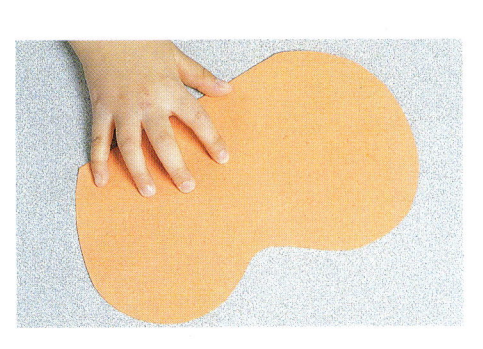 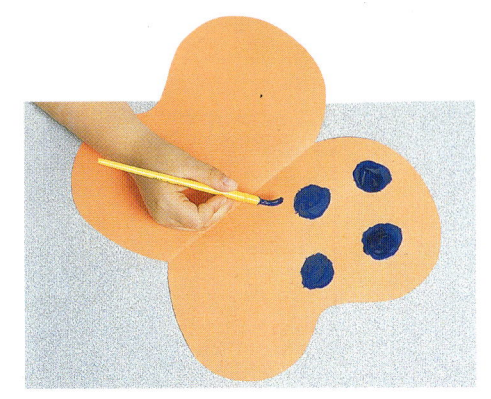

1. Fold a paper butterfly in half.

2. On one side, paint some dots.

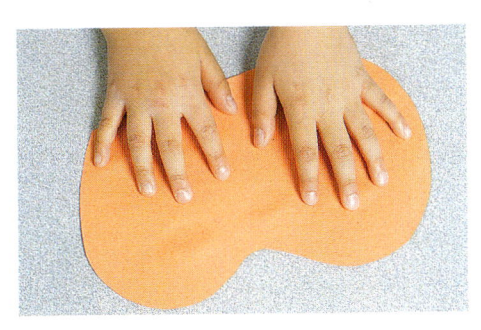 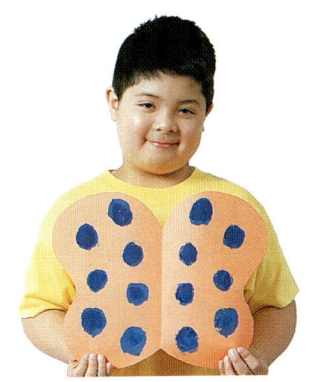

3. Fold your butterfly, and rub it with your hands.

4. Open it up.

The two sides are the same. They match!

Are the sides the same
on a leaf?
Put your finger
in the middle to see.

Yes, the two sides are the same.
They match!

1. Take a paper leaf, and fold it in half.

2. Paint three lines on one side.

3. Fold your leaf,
and rub it with your hands.
4. Open it up.

The two sides are the same.
They match!

Look at each picture.
Do the two sides look the same?

Put your finger in the middle of each thing to find out.

Did you find four things with matching sides? That is symmetry!